WHEN I'M GONE
DEATH PLANNER

THIS BOOK BELONGS TO

TABLE OF CONTENTS

My Personal Details _____ 3

Key Contact _____ 4

Medical Information _____ 5

My Final Wishes _____ 6

My Important Documents _____ 17

Insurance Information _____ 23

My Financial Information _____ 27

Useful Contact _____ 34

Rental Agreement _____ 36

Arrangement for Children _____ 40

Internet Accounts, Emails, Profiles and others stuff _____ 48

Arrangement for Pets _____ 57

Letter for _____ 65

My Personal Wishes _____ 75

My Last Words _____ 81

My Apologies _____ 85

Recommendation for My Funeral _____ 91

My Property _____ 96

Funeral Arrangement _____ 99

Notes _____ 105

Answer Question before death _____ 107

Thank you _____ 109

MY PERSONAL DETAILS

Full Name

Date and place of Birth

Social Security Number

Address

City

Marital Status Single ☐ Married ☐ Divorced ☐ Other ☐

Father's Name

Date of Death

Mother's Name

Date of Death

National Insurance Number

National Health Number

Passport Number

Driving License Number

I am an organ donor Yes ☐ No ☐

Financial stutus:

☐ Employed   ☐ Unemployed   ☐ Entrepreneur
☐ Small business owner
☐ Other: _____

KEY CONTACTS

Full Name

Relationship

Phone Number

Address

Email Address

Other Information

MEDICAL INFORMATION

Blood Type _____

Medical Insurance Provider _____

Medical Insurance Number _____

Hospital _____   **Contact** _____

Clinic _____   **Contact** _____

Doctor _____   **Contact** _____

My illnesses _____

_____

_____

_____

_____

_____

Others Information _____

_____

_____

_____

FINAL WISHES

Legal Name:

Maiden Name:

Phone Number:

Date of Birth:

Place of Birth

Home Address:

Occupation:

Name of Beneficiary:

Name of Attorney

LOCATION DOCUMENTS

My will or trust is located:

My keys are located:

My life insurance paperwork is located:

My bank statement are located:

FINAL WISHES

Legal Name:

Maiden Name:

Phone Number:

Date of Birth:

Place of Birth

Home Address:

Occupation:

Name of Beneficiary:

Name of Attorney

LOCATION DOCUMENTS

My will or trust is located:

My keys are located:

My life insurance paperwork is located:

My bank statement are located:

FINAL WISHES

Legal Name:

Maiden Name:

Phone Number:

Date of Birth:

Place of Birth

Home Address:

Occupation:

Name of Beneficiary:

Name of Attorney

LOCATION DOCUMENTS

My will or trust is located:

My keys are located:

My life insurance paperwork is located:

My bank statement are located:

FINAL WISHES

Legal Name:

Maiden Name:

Phone Number:

Date of Birth:

Place of Birth

Home Address:

Occupation:

Name of Beneficiary:

Name of Attorney

LOCATION DOCUMENTS

My will or trust is located:

My keys are located:

My life insurance paperwork is located:

My bank statement are located:

FINAL WISHES

Legal Name:

Maiden Name:

Phone Number:

Date of Birth:

Place of Birth

Home Address:

Occupation:

Name of Beneficiary:

Name of Attorney

LOCATION DOCUMENTS

My will or trust is located:

My keys are located:

My life insurance paperwork is located:

My bank statement are located:

FINAL WISHES

Legal Name:

Maiden Name:

Phone Number:

Date of Birth:

Place of Birth

Home Address:

Occupation:

Name of Beneficiary:

Name of Attorney

LOCATION DOCUMENTS

My will or trust is located:

My keys are located:

My life insurance paperwork is located:

My bank statement are located:

FINAL WISHES

Legal Name:

Maiden Name:

Phone Number:

Date of Birth:

Place of Birth

Home Address:

Occupation:

Name of Beneficiary:

Name of Attorney

LOCATION DOCUMENTS

My will or trust is located:

My keys are located:

My life insurance paperwork is located:

My bank statement are located:

FINAL WISHES

Legal Name:

Maiden Name:

Phone Number:

Date of Birth:

Place of Birth

Home Address:

Occupation:

Name of Beneficiary:

Name of Attorney

LOCATION DOCUMENTS

My will or trust is located:

My keys are located:

My life insurance paperwork is located:

My bank statement are located:

FINAL WISHES

Legal Name:

Maiden Name:

Phone Number:

Date of Birth:

Place of Birth

Home Address:

Occupation:

Name of Beneficiary:

Name of Attorney

LOCATION DOCUMENTS

My will or trust is located:

My keys are located:

My life insurance paperwork is located:

My bank statement are located:

FINAL WISHES

Legal Name:

Maiden Name:

Phone Number:

Date of Birth:

Place of Birth

Home Address:

Occupation:

Name of Beneficiary:

Name of Attorney

LOCATION DOCUMENTS

My will or trust is located:

My keys are located:

My life insurance paperwork is located:

My bank statement are located:

FINAL WISHES

Legal Name:

Maiden Name:

Phone Number:

Date of Birth:

Place of Birth

Home Address:

Occupation:

Name of Beneficiary:

Name of Attorney

LOCATION DOCUMENTS

My will or trust is located:

My keys are located:

My life insurance paperwork is located:

My bank statement are located:

MY IMPORTANT DOCUMENTS

Documents _____

Location _____

What to do _____

_____

MY EXECUTORS ARE:

Full Name _____

Address _____

Phone Number _____

E-mail _____

Full Name _____

Address _____

Phone Number _____

E-mail _____

MY IMPORTANT DOCUMENTS

Documents _____

Location _____

What to do _____

_____

MY EXECUTORS ARE:

Full Name _____

Address _____

Phone Number _____

E-mail _____

Full Name _____

Address _____

Phone Number _____

E-mail _____

MY IMPORTANT DOCUMENTS

Documents _____

Location _____

What to do _____

MY EXECUTORS ARE:

Full Name _____

Address _____

Phone Number _____

E-mail _____

Full Name _____

Address _____

Phone Number _____

E-mail _____

MY IMPORTANT DOCUMENTS

Documents _____

Location _____

What to do _____

_____

MY EXECUTORS ARE:

Full Name _____

Address _____

Phone Number _____

E-mail _____

Full Name _____

Address _____

Phone Number _____

E-mail _____

MY IMPORTANT DOCUMENTS

Documents _____

Location _____

What to do _____

_____

MY EXECUTORS ARE:

Full Name _____

Address _____

Phone Number _____

E-mail _____

Full Name _____

Address _____

Phone Number _____

E-mail _____

MY IMPORTANT DOCUMENTS

Documents _____

Location _____

What to do _____

_____

MY EXECUTORS ARE:

Full Name _____

Address _____

Phone Number _____

E-mail _____

Full Name _____

Address _____

Phone Number _____

E-mail _____

INSURANCE INFORMATION

INSURANCE DETAILS:

- **Insurance Type:**
- **Company/Agency:**
- **Agent:**
- **Phone:**
- **Email:**
- **Notes:**

INSURANCE DETAILS:

- **Insurance Type:**
- **Company/Agency:**
- **Agent:**
- **Phone:**
- **Email:**
- **Notes:**

INSURANCE INFORMATION

INSURANCE DETAILS:

- **Insurance Type:**
- **Company/Agency:**
- **Agent:**
- **Phone:**
- **Email:**
- **Notes:**

INSURANCE DETAILS:

- **Insurance Type:**
- **Company/Agency:**
- **Agent:**
- **Phone:**
- **Email:**
- **Notes:**

INSURANCE INFORMATION

INSURANCE DETAILS:

Insurance Type:

Company/Agency:

Agent:

Phone:

Email:

Notes:

INSURANCE DETAILS:

Insurance Type:

Company/Agency:

Agent:

Phone:

Email:

Notes:

INSURANCE INFORMATION

INSURANCE DETAILS:

Insurance Type:

Company/Agency:

Agent:

Phone:

Email:

Notes:

INSURANCE DETAILS:

Insurance Type:

Company/Agency:

Agent:

Phone:

Email:

Notes:

MY FINANCIAL DETAILS

BANK ACCOUNT & CREDIT CARDS

- **Account Number:**
- **Account Holder Name:**
- **Credit Card Type**
- **Card User name**
- **Card Password**
- **Expiration date:**

CURRENT ACCOUNT:

- **Account Number:**
- **Account Holder Name:**
- **Credit Card Type**
- **Card User name**
- **Card Password**
- **Expiration date:**

MY FINANCIAL DETAILS

BANK ACCOUNT & CREDIT CARDS

Account Number:
Account Holder Name:
Credit Card Type
Card User name
Card Password
Expiration date:

CURRENT ACCOUNT:

Account Number:
Account Holder Name:
Credit Card Type
Card User name
Card Password
Expiration date:

MY FINANCIAL DETAILS

BANK ACCOUNT & CREDIT CARDS

Account Number:

Account Holder Name:

Credit Card Type

Card User name

Card Password

Expiration date:

CURRENT ACCOUNT:

Account Number:

Account Holder Name:

Credit Card Type

Card User name

Card Password

Expiration date:

MY FINANCIAL DETAILS

BANK ACCOUNT & CREDIT CARDS

Account Number:

Account Holder Name:

Credit Card Type

Card User name

Card Password

Expiration date:

CURRENT ACCOUNT:

Account Number:

Account Holder Name:

Credit Card Type

Card User name

Card Password

Expiration date:

MY FINANCIAL DETAILS

BANK ACCOUNT & CREDIT CARDS

- **Account Number:**
- **Account Holder Name:**
- **Credit Card Type**
- **Card User name**
- **Card Password**
- **Expiration date:**

CURRENT ACCOUNT:

- **Account Number:**
- **Account Holder Name:**
- **Credit Card Type**
- **Card User name**
- **Card Password**
- **Expiration date:**

MY FINANCIAL DETAILS

BANK ACCOUNT & CREDIT CARDS

Account Number:

Account Holder Name:

Credit Card Type

Card User name

Card Password

Expiration date:

CURRENT ACCOUNT:

Account Number:

Account Holder Name:

Credit Card Type

Card User name

Card Password

Expiration date:

MY FINANCIAL DETAILS

BANK ACCOUNT & CREDIT CARDS

- **Account Number:**
- **Account Holder Name:**
- **Credit Card Type**
- **Card User name**
- **Card Password**
- **Expiration date:**

CURRENT ACCOUNT:

- **Account Number:**
- **Account Holder Name:**
- **Credit Card Type**
- **Card User name**
- **Card Password**
- **Expiration date:**

USEFUL CONTACT

ATTORNEYS:

Name:
Phone:
Email:
Address:

DOCTOR:

Name:
Phone:
Email:
Address:

RELATIVES

Name:
Phone:
Email:
Address:

FRIENDS

Name:
Phone:
Email:
Address:

USEFUL CONTACT

ATTORNEYS:

Name:
Phone:
Email:
Address:

DOCTOR:

Name:
Phone:
Email:
Address:

RELATIVES

Name:
Phone:
Email:
Address:

FRIENDS

Name:
Phone:
Email:
Address:

RENTAL AGREEMENT

RENTAL UNIT LOCATION:

Address:

Parties:

Homeowner/Principal Tenant (Circle)   Tenant:

Name (Print & Signature)   Name (Print & Signature)

Terms:

Length of Agreement (Circle):   One year   Month to Month   Other: _____

Rent:

$_____. payable monthly on the _____ day of the month, made payable to _____ Rent ____ Does ____ does not include utilities. If it does, utility payments will go as follows:

        Gas/Electricity: Tenant pays _____ % of monthly bill.
        Water/Garbage: Tenant pays _____ % of monthly bill.
        Other _____: Tenant pays _____ % of monthly bill.

Late fee of $_____ will apply if payment is not made by above date

Deposit:

        Last month's rent: Paid on _____ Amount $ _____
        Security deposit: Paid on _____ Amount $ _____

        Gas/Electricity: Tenant pays _____ % of monthly bill.
        Water/Garbage: Tenant pays _____ % of monthly bill.
        Other _____: Tenant pays _____ % of monthly bill.

RENTAL AGREEMENT

RENTAL UNIT LOCATION:

Address:

Parties:

Homeowner/Principal Tenant (Circle)   Tenant:

Name (Print & Signature)   Name (Print & Signature)

Terms:

Length of Agreement (Circle):   One year   Month to Month   Other: _____

Rent:

$_____. payable monthly on the _____ day of the month, made payable to _____ Rent ____ Does ____ does not include utilities. If it does, utility payments will go as follows:

      Gas/Electricity: Tenant pays _____ % of monthly bill.
      Water/Garbage: Tenant pays _____ % of monthly bill.
      Other _____: Tenant pays _____ % of monthly bill.

Late fee of $_____ will apply if payment is not made by above date

Deposit:

Last month's rent: Paid on _____ Amount $ _____
Security deposit: Paid on _____ Amount $ _____

      Gas/Electricity: Tenant pays _____ % of monthly bill.
      Water/Garbage: Tenant pays _____ % of monthly bill.
      Other _____: Tenant pays _____ % of monthly bill.

RENTAL AGREEMENT

RENTAL UNIT LOCATION:

Address:

Parties:

Homeowner/Principal Tenant (Circle)   Tenant:

Name (Print & Signature)   Name (Print & Signature)

Terms:

Length of Agreement (Circle):   One year   Month to Month   Other: _____

Rent:

$_____. payable monthly on the _____ day of the month, made payable to _____ Rent ____ Does ____ does not include utilities. If it does, utility payments will go as follows:

  Gas/Electricity: Tenant pays _____ % of monthly bill.
  Water/Garbage: Tenant pays _____ % of monthly bill.
  Other _____: Tenant pays _____ % of monthly bill.

Late fee of $_____ will apply if payment is not made by above date

Deposit:

  Last month's rent: Paid on _____ Amount $ _____
  Security deposit: Paid on _____ Amount $ _____

  Gas/Electricity: Tenant pays _____ % of monthly bill.
  Water/Garbage: Tenant pays _____ % of monthly bill.
  Other _____: Tenant pays _____ % of monthly bill.

RENTAL AGREEMENT

RENTAL UNIT LOCATION:

Address:

Parties:

Homeowner/Principal Tenant (Circle)   Tenant:

Name (Print & Signature)   Name (Print & Signature)

Terms:

Length of Agreement (Circle):   One year   Month to Month   Other: _____

Rent:

$_____. payable monthly on the _____ day of the month, made payable to _____ Rent ____ Does ____ does not include utilities. If it does, utility payments will go as follows:

   Gas/Electricity: Tenant pays _____ % of monthly bill.
   Water/Garbage: Tenant pays _____ % of monthly bill.
   Other _____: Tenant pays _____ % of monthly bill.

Late fee of $_____ will apply if payment is not made by above date

Deposit:

Last month's rent: Paid on _____ Amount $ _____
Security deposit: Paid on _____ Amount $ _____

   Gas/Electricity: Tenant pays _____ % of monthly bill.
   Water/Garbage: Tenant pays _____ % of monthly bill.
   Other _____: Tenant pays _____ % of monthly bill.

ARRANGEMENT FOR CHILDREN

ARRANGEMENT FOR CHILDREN

ARRANGEMENT FOR CHILDREN

ARRANGEMENT FOR CHILDREN

ARRANGEMENT FOR CHILDREN

ARRANGEMENT FOR CHILDREN

ARRANGEMENT FOR CHILDREN

ARRANGEMENT FOR CHILDREN

INTERNET ACCOUNTS, EMAILS, PROFILES AND OTHER STUFF

EMAIL ACCOUNT:

Email:		Pass:	
Email:		Pass:	
Email:		Pass:	

FB:

| Fb Ac: | | Pass: | |
| Fb Ac: | | Pass: | |

INST:

| Inst Ac: | | Pass: | |
| Inst Ac; | | Pass: | |

TW:

| Tw Ac: | | Pass: | |
| Tw Ac; | | Pass: | |

OTHERS:

Other Ac:		Pass:	
Other Ac;		Pass:	
Other Ac:		Pass:	
Other Ac;		Pass:	
Other Ac:		Pass:	
Other Ac;		Pass:	
Other Ac:		Pass:	
Other Ac;		Pass:	

INTERNET ACCOUNTS, EMAILS, PROFILES AND OTHER STUFF

EMAIL ACCOUNT:

Email:		Pass:	
Email:		Pass:	
Email:		Pass:	

FB:

Fb Ac:		Pass:	
Fb Ac:		Pass:	

INST:

Inst Ac:		Pass:	
Inst Ac;		Pass:	

TW:

Tw Ac:		Pass:	
Tw Ac;		Pass:	

OTHERS:

Other Ac:		Pass:	
Other Ac;		Pass:	
Other Ac:		Pass:	
Other Ac;		Pass:	
Other Ac:		Pass:	
Other Ac;		Pass:	
Other Ac:		Pass:	
Other Ac;		Pass:	

INTERNET ACCOUNTS, EMAILS, PROFILES AND OTHER STUFF

EMAIL ACCOUNT:

Email:		Pass:	
Email:		Pass:	
Email:		Pass:	

FB:

| Fb Ac: | | Pass: | |
| Fb Ac: | | Pass: | |

INST:

| Inst Ac: | | Pass: | |
| Inst Ac; | | Pass: | |

TW:

| Tw Ac: | | Pass: | |
| Tw Ac; | | Pass: | |

OTHERS:

Other Ac:		Pass:	
Other Ac;		Pass:	
Other Ac:		Pass:	
Other Ac;		Pass:	
Other Ac:		Pass:	
Other Ac;		Pass:	
Other Ac:		Pass:	
Other Ac;		Pass:	

INTERNET ACCOUNTS, EMAILS, PROFILES AND OTHER STUFF

EMAIL ACCOUNT:

Email:		Pass:	
Email:		Pass:	
Email:		Pass:	

FB:

| Fb Ac: | | Pass: | |
| Fb Ac: | | Pass: | |

INST:

| Inst Ac: | | Pass: | |
| Inst Ac; | | Pass: | |

TW:

| Tw Ac: | | Pass: | |
| Tw Ac; | | Pass: | |

OTHERS:

Other Ac:		Pass:	
Other Ac;		Pass:	
Other Ac:		Pass:	
Other Ac;		Pass:	
Other Ac:		Pass:	
Other Ac;		Pass:	
Other Ac:		Pass:	
Other Ac;		Pass:	

INTERNET ACCOUNTS, EMAILS, PROFILES AND OTHER STUFF

EMAIL ACCOUNT:

Email:		Pass:	
Email:		Pass:	
Email:		Pass:	

FB:

| Fb Ac: | | Pass: | |
| Fb Ac: | | Pass: | |

INST:

| Inst Ac: | | Pass: | |
| Inst Ac; | | Pass: | |

TW:

| Tw Ac: | | Pass: | |
| Tw Ac; | | Pass: | |

OTHERS:

Other Ac:		Pass:	
Other Ac;		Pass:	
Other Ac:		Pass:	
Other Ac;		Pass:	
Other Ac:		Pass:	
Other Ac;		Pass:	
Other Ac:		Pass:	
Other Ac;		Pass:	

INTERNET ACCOUNTS, EMAILS, PROFILES AND OTHER STUFF

EMAIL ACCOUNT:

Email:		Pass:	
Email:		Pass:	
Email:		Pass:	

FB:

| Fb Ac: | | Pass: | |
| Fb Ac: | | Pass: | |

INST:

| Inst Ac: | | Pass: | |
| Inst Ac; | | Pass: | |

TW:

| Tw Ac: | | Pass: | |
| Tw Ac; | | Pass: | |

OTHERS:

Other Ac:		Pass:	
Other Ac;		Pass:	
Other Ac:		Pass:	
Other Ac;		Pass:	
Other Ac:		Pass:	
Other Ac;		Pass:	
Other Ac:		Pass:	
Other Ac;		Pass:	

INTERNET ACCOUNTS, EMAILS, PROFILES AND OTHER STUFF

EMAIL ACCOUNT:

Email:		Pass:	
Email:		Pass:	
Email:		Pass:	

FB:

| Fb Ac: | | Pass: | |
| Fb Ac: | | Pass: | |

INST:

| Inst Ac: | | Pass: | |
| Inst Ac; | | Pass: | |

TW:

| Tw Ac: | | Pass: | |
| Tw Ac; | | Pass: | |

OTHERS:

Other Ac:		Pass:	
Other Ac;		Pass:	
Other Ac:		Pass:	
Other Ac;		Pass:	
Other Ac:		Pass:	
Other Ac;		Pass:	
Other Ac:		Pass:	
Other Ac;		Pass:	

INTERNET ACCOUNTS, EMAILS, PROFILES AND OTHER STUFF

EMAIL ACCOUNT:
Email:		Pass:	
Email:		Pass:	
Email:		Pass:	

FB:
| Fb Ac: | | Pass: | |
| Fb Ac: | | Pass: | |

INST:
| Inst Ac: | | Pass: | |
| Inst Ac; | | Pass: | |

TW:
| Tw Ac: | | Pass: | |
| Tw Ac; | | Pass: | |

OTHERS:
Other Ac:		Pass:	
Other Ac;		Pass:	
Other Ac:		Pass:	
Other Ac;		Pass:	
Other Ac:		Pass:	
Other Ac;		Pass:	
Other Ac:		Pass:	
Other Ac;		Pass:	

INTERNET ACCOUNTS, EMAILS, PROFILES AND OTHER STUFF

EMAIL ACCOUNT:

Email:		Pass:	
Email:		Pass:	
Email:		Pass:	

FB:

| Fb Ac: | | Pass: | |
| Fb Ac: | | Pass: | |

INST:

| Inst Ac: | | Pass: | |
| Inst Ac; | | Pass: | |

TW:

| Tw Ac: | | Pass: | |
| Tw Ac; | | Pass: | |

OTHERS:

Other Ac:		Pass:	
Other Ac;		Pass:	
Other Ac:		Pass:	
Other Ac;		Pass:	
Other Ac:		Pass:	
Other Ac;		Pass:	
Other Ac:		Pass:	
Other Ac;		Pass:	

ARRANGEMENT FOR PETS

ARRANGEMENT FOR PETS

ARRANGEMENT FOR PETS

ARRANGEMENT FOR PETS

ARRANGEMENT FOR PETS

ARRANGEMENT FOR PETS

ARRANGEMENT FOR PETS

ARRANGEMENT FOR PETS

Letter to: _____

Letter to: _____

Letter to: _____

MY PERSONAL WISHES
for My spouse, my children, my friends, my pets

My Spouse

_____

_____

_____

My Childrens

_____

_____

_____

My Friends

_____

_____

_____

My Pets

_____

MY PERSONAL WISHES
for My spouse, my children, my friends, my pets

My Spouse

_____
_____
_____

My Childrens

_____
_____
_____

My Friends

_____
_____
_____

My Pets

_____

MY PERSONAL WISHES
for My spouse, my children, my friends, my pets

My Spouse

_____
_____
_____

My Childrens

_____
_____
_____

My Friends

_____
_____
_____

My Pets

_____

MY PERSONAL WISHES
for My spouse, my children, my friends, my pets

My Spouse

_____

_____

_____

_____

My Childrens

_____

_____

_____

_____

My Friends

_____

_____

_____

_____

My Pets

_____

MY PERSONAL WISHES
for My spouse, my children, my friends, my pets

My Spouse

_____
_____
_____

My Childrens

_____
_____
_____

My Friends

_____
_____
_____

My Pets

_____

MY PERSONAL WISHES
for My spouse, my children, my friends, my pets

My Spouse

_____

_____

_____

My Childrens

_____

_____

_____

My Friends

_____

_____

_____

My Pets

_____

MY LAST WORDS

MY LAST WORDS

MY LAST WORDS

MY LAST WORDS

MY APOLOGIES

MY APOLOGIES

MY APOLOGIES

MY APOLOGIES

MY APOLOGIES

MY APOLOGIES

RECOMMENDATION FOR MY FUNERAL

RECOMMENDATION FOR MY FUNERAL

RECOMMENDATION FOR MY FUNERAL

RECOMMENDATION FOR MY FUNERAL

RECOMMENDATION FOR MY FUNERAL

MY PROPERTY

Type:
Location:
Co-owner:
Year of Acquisition

Type:
Location:
Co-owner:
Year of Acquisition

Attorneys

Document:
Location:
What to Do:

MY PROPERTY

Type:

Location:

Co-owner:

Year of Acquisition

Type:

Location:

Co-owner:

Year of Acquisition

Attorneys

Document:

Location:

What to Do:

MY PROPERTY

Type:
Location:
Co-owner:
Year of Acquisition

Type:
Location:
Co-owner:
Year of Acquisition

Attorneys

Document:
Location:
What to Do:

FUNERAL ARRANGEMENT

Family Members:

Funeral Home:

Contact No:

Funeral Wishes

Information Attached (If Applicable)

Funeral Arrangment

Family Members:

Burial _____   Cremation _____

Burial Plot Information / Ashes Location

Information Attached (If Applicable)

FUNERAL ARRANGEMENT

Family Members:

Funeral Home:

Contact No:

Funeral Wishes

Information Attached (If Applicable)

Funeral Arrangment

Family Members:

Burial _____   Cremation _____

Burial Plot Information / Ashes Location

Information Attached (If Applicable)

FUNERAL ARRANGEMENT

Family Members:

Funeral Home:

Contact No:

Funeral Wishes

Information Attached (If Applicable)

Funeral Arrangment

Family Members:

Burial _____   Cremation _____

Burial Plot Information / Ashes Location

Information Attached (If Applicable)

FUNERAL ARRANGEMENT

Family Members:

Funeral Home:

Contact No:

Funeral Wishes

Information Attached (If Applicable)

Funeral Arrangment

Family Members:

Burial _____   Cremation _____

Burial Plot Information / Ashes Location

Information Attached (If Applicable)

FUNERAL ARRANGEMENT

Family Members:

Funeral Home:

Contact No:

Funeral Wishes

Information Attached (If Applicable)

Funeral Arrangment

Family Members:

Burial _____   Cremation _____

Burial Plot Information / Ashes Location

Information Attached (If Applicable)

FUNERAL ARRANGEMENT

Family Members:

Funeral Home:

Contact No:

Funeral Wishes

Information Attached (If Applicable)

Funeral Arrangment

Family Members:

Burial _____   **Cremation** _____

Burial Plot Information / Ashes Location

Information Attached (If Applicable)

NOTES

DATE: / /

NOTES

DATE: / /

Answer Question Before Death Planner

Q.No.1

If I was to die today, what would I regret not doing?

Q.No.2

What will matter to me most when I am on my deathbed?

Q.No.3

What would my last meal request be?

Q.No.4

What am I most proud of?

Q.No.5

Will I donate my organs?

Answer Question Before Death Planner

Q.No.1

What can I learn from the death of a loved one?

Q.No.2

Am I afraid of death?

Q.No.3

What is my biggest achievement in my life?

Q.No.4

What is my weakness?

Q.No.5

Which place I want to visit again in my life?

Thank you!

_____
Signature

Made in United States
Troutdale, OR
09/27/2024

23204067R00062